RELIGIOUS EDUCATION

IN KEY STAGE 1

A PRACTICAL GUIDE

RELIGIOUS EDUCATION

IN KEY STAGE 1

A PRACTICAL GUIDE

Terence and Gill Copley

SOUTHGATE

First published 1993 by Southgate Publishers Ltd

Southgate Publishers Ltd
Glebe House, Church Street, Crediton,
Devon EX17 2AF

Printed and bound in Great Britain by
Short Run Press Ltd, Exeter, Devon

British Library Cataloguing in Publication Data
A CIP catalogue record for this book is available from
the British Library.

ISBN 1–85741–046–7

ACKNOWLEDGEMENTS

Photographs are reproduced by permission of the
following:

Britain Israel Public Affairs Centre p.38
G. Bodrov/Hutchison Library p.42
D. Brinicombe/Hutchison Library p.43 (R)
J. Pate/Hutchison Library p.35
Sarah Thorley pp.31, 36, 43(L), 44, 46
Deborah Martin p.23
The photograph on p.14 was taken at St Sidwell's
Combined School; other photographs were taken at
Withycombe Raleigh Primary School.

The material on pp. 26, 27, 40, 47–51 is reproduced
from *The FARE Report.*

CONTENTS

INTRODUCTION

Some infant teachers have understandable reservations when it comes to teaching RE. They may wonder whether it is better left until the children are older and able to grasp the seemingly difficult or abstract ideas of religion. Some teachers may feel inadequate in their own knowledge and training for RE. Some may be unsure about their own personal beliefs and dis-beliefs and feel hesitant about embarking on what they see as the transmission of religious beliefs and values in the class-room. In contrast, those who are sure about their own beliefs recognise that there is a danger of undue influence of their beliefs on the children they teach.

For others the sheer pressure of imple-menting the National Curriculum and associated testing means that RE is being pushed out through lack of time in the working lives of desperately busy teachers. It is tempting to leave it to the vicar's visit in assembly and the annual preparations for Christmas and to tell oneself that these ensure that somehow RE is being done.

Another way of making Key Stage 1 RE disappear is when it is claimed that infant RE is 'everywhere in the curriculum'. In such cases it can be hard to find it in any recognisable form anywhere. However, after the 1988 Education Reform Act, the law requires us to be able to identify where teaching and learning in RE has occurred, so this 'everywhere and nowhere' approach is no longer acceptable.

Meanwhile children persist in raising their own religious – or at any rate 'deep' – issues, sometimes in the form of state-ments rather than questions.

Grandma's gone to be with Jesus.
It was nasty of God to send the rain. (After the Noah story.)

Where is God?
Will there be an end of days?

Infants will even debate religion.

It was magic.
She was really there.
Is it real?
I don't believe it.
(After a unit of work including a vision.)

And small children seem to have an innate sense of wonder and reverence for life and an ability to see it whole, an awareness that by adolescence and adulthood – or even Key Stage 2! – has often disappeared. As they grow up they will be constantly forming impressions about religion from the media and from festivals such as Christmas and Easter or perhaps Ramadan, Divali or Passover, including festival greetings cards, gifts and parties. Small children may be taken to marriage ceremonies or religious ceremonies associ-ated with birth or initiation: these too make their impression.

Then there are the doorstep salespeople of religious sects, trying to impress their beliefs upon the person visited or – per-haps the biggest indoctrination of all – the contaminating effect of adult indifference. The prevalent mood among many adults is that 'Religion doesn't really matter very much, does it?' Religion is seen as a hobby of a tiny and often fanatical minority.

It is said that few go to Sunday school or church or mosque or synagogue or tem-ple in our society. Shops are open on Sunday now and the disappearance of the Victorian 'sabbath' is almost complete. It is assumed by many adults without ques-tion or conscious thought that religion is on the way out and their children will 'catch' this indifference just as surely as they may catch a faith.

But is religion doomed? Or could it be like a slump in the economy that bottoms out?! And are we right to identify commitment to religion with attachment to a religious institution such as a church or a mosque or a temple? Sales of religious books have never been higher (until the last recession), so even if commitment to religion has declined, interest in it hasn't. There is also a wider scene than merely the UK. If religion appears to be a matter of indifference in our secular western culture, that is not the case across the world as a whole. In the global village religion is alive and well, and in some places growing fast (even some places in the UK). Indeed, some of the prejudice against Muslims in Britain might relate to their strong and articulate presence in our society.

We fail our children if we don't offer them some help and insight, even at infant level, into religion, and if we don't share their own questions and comments with them. Teaching children about religion is not the same as trying to force it on them. It is not the same as claiming that we personally hold all the answers. It is about sharing curiosity and questions and exploring some of the answers that humankind has come up with over thousands of years. To opt out, for whatever reason, by failing to teach about religion is in the long run to reduce our children's choices. And reducing people's choice is what indoctrination is all about.

Finally, we need to remember that religion has never been the exclusive possession of the specialist, whether the specialist teacher, or the professional religious priest or rabbi or the full-time leader of a faith community, respected and important though they may be. It has a place among ordinary people. The non-specialist should not therefore be put off. With sensitivity and careful preparation, RE can be taught to infants by their class teacher.

This is why we go on to examine the role of the teacher in RE, what the law says, how to deliver RE within the curriculum, practical examples of infant RE and possible pitfalls. This book is intended to help teachers present RE effectively and enjoy it in the process! When that happens, teacher and pupils will want to learn more.

NOTE

This book is written for students in training, individual teachers who want to improve their competence in RE, and groups of teachers, perhaps using school-based training to tackle their RE together or to draw up proposed policy on RE for their school. With group users in view, sections headed **To think about** have been included. We hope these will be found useful by individuals as well.

ME – TEACH RE?

Teachers of infants come to RE with most of the practical skills needed to do it successfully. They already use story. They are already experienced if not expert at art and craft, at display and topic book work, at question and answer and discussion with their children, at assessing and evaluating children's work within the National Curriculum. With all this expertise, why are some uneasy about teaching it?

The answer is sometimes a crisis of conscience, more often a crisis of content – knowing what to teach and the right way in. We look at how to select and use suitable content in most of the rest of this book. Here we are concerned with the first possible stumbling block, the matter of conscience. The teacher sometimes assumes that she must be teaching religion – whatever the religion in question happens to be – as if it were 'true', when maybe she doesn't think it is or she just isn't sure. Therefore the easy way out is to duck the issue. She chooses to do 'caring and sharing' instead, and thereby opt out of RE and into Personal and Social Education. Of course, the great religions of the world believe in caring and sharing, but this is rarely pointed out to children, and in any case these faiths believe in lots more things as well: their members aren't merely 'good' people whose existence is spent caring and sharing! Personal and Social Education has its proper place, but it isn't the same as Religious Education, for in PSE the 'R' bit has disappeared.

Teachers of infants already use the skills of storytelling and discussion which are a vital part of successful RE teaching.

It helps to see RE as arising out of the contact points between three areas.

The needs, questions and experience of the child

Children already have impressions of religion forming in their minds and experiences of life which can be more adult – and searing – than many adults imagine. They will also have begun to raise the sort of 'deep' question or remark to which we referred on p.5. As they grow up they may be faced with choice in religion. This is seldom, if ever, the choice between being a Buddhist or a Hindu or a Christian or a Muslim. Such choices are exceptional, even at adult level. Rather the choices will be between the religion of their culture or family, if the family has a religion, and between agnosticism (the 'don't know' vote) and atheism (the 'no' vote).

Most teachers see education as being concerned with choice and understanding, rather than instruction and transmission, so religious education will open up not so much choices between religions, but the choice between a religious and a non-religious way of life. As we have seen, without RE many children will grow up with no real choice at all. They will have been 'brainwashed' by our secular culture just as effectively as the apparent fanatics from religiously based republics who appear on television have been 'brainwashed' by their culture.

The experience of the teacher

Teachers will have already had experience of religious education – their own at school – that may have been good, bad, or in between, and they may have had experience of a religion as well. They may have been to church, Sunday school, synagogue, mosque class or whatever. They may have strong feelings for or against religion or a particular religion. They may have been converted to a religion, or discarded one.

What this means is that no teacher approaches religion from a position of neutrality. We all approach it from a position of belief, or uncertainty or scepticism. Becoming aware of that and being honest about it is the first step to teaching RE successfully. Adults and children have had experiences of living which the great religions have addressed: we have loved and perhaps lost, grieved and sorrowed, seen birth and death, and sometimes wondered at it or about it. We have found the questions and answers and attitudes of religion helpful, or not.

The wisdom and experience of the great world faiths

Whether we happen to be religious or not, we might be humble enough to acknowledge that, culturally speaking, the great world faiths have an accumulation of human wisdom and experience in addressing the questions faced by humanity over thousands of years. They have things to say about love and hate, creation and destiny, forgiveness and punishment, God and people, women and men, sex, marriage and divorce, war and peace, meaning and purpose.

Of course, this does not make all – or even any – of their statements 'true' or 'right', but it does mean that they provide parables, story, history and direct teaching in these areas that impinge on the experiences and questions of adults and children, even very young children.

As teachers we need to 'tap into' the experiences and views arrived at by these faiths that might be relevant to our children.

So when we prepare to teach RE we need to be aware of those three areas that will influence our teaching.

We can then go on to identify certain principles which should provide us with the confidence that it is right and urgent to tackle this subject and that we can attempt RE with a clear conscience in the infant classroom.

Principles

- We as teachers have an absolute right to our personal religious belief, whatever it is, or to our uncertainty or our disbelief.

- The children we teach have an absolute right to their beliefs and disbeliefs, but also, and equally important, the right to learn more about this whole area of human experience so their eventual stance in these matters is not founded on ignorance and prejudice.

- Trying to persuade children of the rightness of a particular religion is the province of the home and family, the church, the temple, etc. rather than the teacher.

- The teacher's role when dealing with religion is to do with promoting tolerance, dispelling ignorance, raising questions, and introducing children to new ways of looking at life and to the experiences of other people.

- In order to do this we have to be honest with ourselves and keep our own beliefs and disbeliefs under control in the classroom, so that while we may feel in honesty that at some point we need to declare them to children, we shall try not to inflict them upon the youngsters. This will be hard because in the infant classroom 'Miss' is always right. 'Miss' therefore needs to provide balance: X thinks this ... Y thinks that ... and so on. Establishing a distinction between teaching and preaching applies whether we are in danger of preaching agnosticism, atheism or a religious belief.

- In a religiously founded school – Christian, Jewish or more recently Muslim – the school may be seen by teachers and parents as a sort of extended family or faith community and will be allowed or encouraged to devote some of its time to nurturing children in the faith of that community. But we note that the children in these schools have the same educational needs as the children in all schools and much of what has been said above about RE will still apply to them.

- In teaching any subject well, we have to be committed to it being educationally worthwhile and interesting; that applies to RE. We don't have to be religious to teach it and religious teachers may occasionally find it hard not to evangelise the class, but we do have to be ready to deal with religion and religious options on questions of meaning. Otherwise a fear of indoctrinating children into religion may lead to a silence that indoctrinates them out of it.

Developing attitudes

Rightly developed, these principles will help teachers to develop through RE particular attitudes in children. It should be emphasized that these are attitudes rather than beliefs. Children will decide for themselves what they believe as they grow older. But developing attitudes is part of teaching any subject; love of music and music making or of literature and writing or analytical enquiry are some of the attitudes some other subjects might aim to foster. For RE they may include:

- awareness of our needs and the needs of others and how we might respond;

- tolerance and respect, which involves understanding that people have different views about things and take different things seriously, so that there isn't always just one 'right' answer;

- curiosity towards religions, which involves understanding that they are full of interest and variety and they have things to say about situations encountered by people of all ages;

- awareness that there is often more to life than at first appears;

- understanding that religions are alive and not museum pieces and that they

say things about what human beings are like and what they can become;

- understanding that however we choose to talk about 'him' or 'her', or whether we dispense with the idea altogether, 'God' is taken seriously by many people in many religions worldwide.

TO THINK ABOUT

RE in school policy

1. Is there a consensus among staff in the school you know best on the nature and aims of RE?

2. What statement about RE appears in the publications of the school you know best and how far does it meet the issues raised above?

3. In a church voluntary aided – or other religiously based – school, what do you think should be the right balance between the educational needs of the children for 'open' RE and the requirements of nurture within a family of faith? How are these different requirements best met? (Collective worship, RE lessons, the whole ethos of the school, pastoral arrangements, religious festivals, etc.)

RE as an experience for children

4. Looking back, can you remember any of the RE you experienced as a child? What was good or bad about it?

5. How far should we tell young children about our own religious views?

6. At one time it was thought that primary schools should lay a religious, usually Christian, foundation so that children had something rather than nothing to reject or accept in adulthood. This was based on the grounds that we live in not so much a Christian country as a broadly Christian culture. How far can this view be held now?

Awe and wonder in RE

Young children, especially pre-school and infant children, have a sense of awe and wonder that can be lost as they get older. The ungracious jeering or bored-with-everything characteristics put on by some adolescents seem to suppress wonder fairly well!

Awe and wonder arise in spontaneous experiences and can never be conscripted. They may be part of religious experience, but neither is inevitably religious. Creating circumstances in which awe and wonder might arise and giving space to them when they occur is perhaps addressing the 1988 Act requirement that we be concerned with the spiritual education of children, something the Act doesn't define. We need to allow the child to express wonder whenever in the curriculum it arises: Science, Art, Drama, Technology, RE, etc.

Do awe and wonder constitute RE? Because they can occur in any subject or at any time, they are no substitute for the RE syllabus and programme but they may enhance learning in any subject, RE included. Nor would we wish to forget that there are some things outside the National and Basic Curriculum that are still worthwhile!

7. In a given week in your class, record any questions the children raise with you about religious or 'deep' issues and record any occasions on which you choose to raise these issues with them.

8. Do you think small children are naturally or innately religious? On what grounds do you reach your conclusion?

THE LAW AND RE

What the 1988 Education Reform Act and the DES Circular 3/89 say about RE

(This provision applies to England and Wales. Scotland and Northern Ireland are regulated separately.)

- It is religious *education*, where before it had usually been called *instruction*.

- It must be provided for all pupils as a part of the basic curriculum.

- It should have equal standing with National Curriculum subjects.

- It will continue to be locally determined and not subject to nationally prescribed attainment targets and programmes of study.

- In county schools and voluntary controlled schools it will be taught according to an *agreed syllabus*, drawn up by the LEA following a conference of four committees: the LEA, the teachers, the Church of England (except in LEAs in Wales, where there is no 'established' church) and other denominations and faiths represented in the area. Each committee has one collective vote.

- In voluntary aided schools (some of the church or other religion schools) RE is to be determined by the governors in accordance with the trust deed.

- Parents retain the right to withdraw their child from RE; this includes withdrawing from the premises to receive RE elsewhere. (The Act also has other details concerning withdrawal.)

- There is to be an established complaints procedure which may involve the local Standing Advisory Council for RE. This body has to be set up to advise the LEA on RE and collective worship and may choose to introduce a new agreed syllabus by majority vote of its four committees, formed as above.

- The right of teachers to decline to teach RE is upheld.

- An unqualified teacher (it doesn't mean a non-specialist teacher, but someone with no teaching qualification) may be employed to teach RE only where it is not possible to recruit a qualified teacher to do so.

- In county schools RE shall be non-denominational, but teaching *about* denominations is permitted.

What the Act doesn't lay down

- How RE shall be taught and organised at school level, though when primary schools do it in integrated work, rather than in identifiable topics or subject slots, it has to be possible for parents to exercise the right of withdrawal.

- What shall be taught, though new agreed syllabuses have been given a planning framework that they must 'reflect the fact that religious traditions in the country are in the main Christian whilst taking account of the teaching and practices of other principal religions'.

- Attainment targets, programmes of study and assessment procedures, though if these are built into the agreed syllabus they become binding at the local level of that syllabus.

Agreed syllabus

These local but binding syllabuses take their odd-sounding name from the requirement that they shall be agreed between the various 'colleges' in the agreed syllabus standing conference: the LEA, teachers, the Church of England (in England) and the other faiths and denominations. Sometimes the prescriptive part of the syllabus is quite short – perhaps a booklet of twenty pages – but many syllabuses offer an accompanying handbook of ideas, useful addresses, etc. to help teachers implement the actual syllabus.

Since teachers constitute only one college out of the four, it looks as if they are in a minority in defining what goes into these syllabuses. (It is worth noting that this still allows them more say than they have in the National Curriculum subjects.) However, the churches and other faith groups often put teacher members on to their panels, so there may well be more teachers involved than those sitting on the teachers' panel. Teachers' panels will usually carry representatives from each key stage.

Assessment

Where an assessment scheme is built in to an agreed syllabus, with attainment targets, programmes of study, etc., these then become as binding as the national ones for other subjects. The difference is that they are devised and administered locally and the chances are that serving teachers at each key stage have had more part in drawing them up and piloting them.

The FARE scheme (Forms of Assessment in Religious Education), which was drawn up for south western LEAs by a team working at Exeter University, involved several hundred teachers in their client LEAs in discussion and in piloting units. In various adapted forms their findings have been built into new agreed syllabuses or agreed syllabus revision in the

FARE LEAs from 1992 onwards. FARE identified two attainment targets:

Reflection on meaning
Knowledge and understanding of religion

Each target addresses three areas of study, with associated programmes of study and specific objectives in each key stage. The report contains 33 pages of practical examples of assessment in Key Stage 1. Similar approaches have been developed elsewhere, notably at Birmingham at the Regional RE Centre at Westhill College. In another scheme, Essex LEA adopted four RE ATs:

Understanding belief
The importance and meaning of belief
The influence of belief
Responses to belief

To many primary teachers, being landed with assessment in RE on top of everything else seems like the last straw, but the experience of teachers working on FARE was that it raised the profile of RE in their schools, brought it on to the staff training map, and helped to improve their own approach and quality in teaching.

There is, of course, a very significant postscript to this, and that is that RE material can be used to help meet attainment targets in other subjects as well.

Examples of ATs that might be met by using some of the topics and follow-up work suggested in Chapter 4	
English	ATs 1, 2 and 3
Geography	AT 2 Level 3 AT 4 Level 1
History	AT 2 Levels 1 – 3
Science	AT 3 Level 3 AT 4 Level 3
Technology	ATs 2 and 3 (the Noah follow-up!)
Art	ATs 1 and 2 (especially 1)

DELIVERING THE GOODS IN THE CLASSROOM

In the infant classroom RE may be delivered in different ways. It is possible, though unlikely, that it will be a timetabled slot, rather like the programmed use of the hall for PE. While that theoretically guarantees the weekly – or more frequent – appearance of the subject, it is too cramping an approach for most infant teachers. Much more likely is that RE will appear in topic work. This will in practice occur in one of two ways:

(a) in an RE-led topic
Certainly it would be reasonable to expect various RE-led topics to appear throughout a year (suggestions are given below). In this case one would expect that the RE part would lead or drive the topic and be at the heart of the planning flow diagram or 'spider' from which Maths, Technology, Science, language work, etc. would flow when their contributions were mapped. It would have a clear 'R' element that would distinguish it from PSE or other subjects; it might address ATs for RE where they are in force; it would dominate eventual display; the content might well address ATs in other subjects as well; there might be an RE-specific assessment procedure at the end. The topic might be derived from the agreed syllabus, or from the samples in Chapter 4 here, or from other published materials such as the Birmingham 'RISC' Project (see Further Reading, p.59).

Topic work is a familiar part of the infant classroom and can easily be used for RE, perhaps as part of a cross-curricular theme or as an RE- led topic.

(b) RE as part of a topic led by another subject theme or a multi-subject or cross-curricular theme

In this case the school will probably have an existing topic bank, perhaps referenced to non-RE ATs, and might be doing one major topic per half term. Here RE will be one of the supporting subjects on the topic map. But it will still have to contain a demonstrable 'R' element to meet the law. Tenuous connections between the topic and religion are to be avoided. A major topic on 'Flight' should not produce an RE spin-off on angels! If RE is 'forced' to fit in to topics in this sort of way, what children would learn over a year would be hit and miss, and marginal to any real understanding of religion. But where there are genuine connections, they should be followed, and in Chapter 4 we have looked at examples of these. In such a situation there may not be major development of the RE beyond story or visit and recording, but as long as there is a balance of RE-led topics in addition to those in which RE provides a subsidiary element, this is no disaster.

A few pressured headteachers have attempted to claim that RE is being delivered in their school through collective worship. Under pressure, people will say anything! Collective worship (assemblies) cannot deliver RE because its aims are different and its audience wider in most schools than the one class.

The content of an agreed syllabus could not be covered in this way, nor would one dream of delivering history or science through worship. The law and educational practice see them as two things, not one. Besides, in some primary schools collective worship itself seems to have become dominated by secular moralising. Not all infant schools sing songs or hymns or say prayers in assemblies any more. Whether this is a good or bad thing is open to debate, but in schools where they do all these things, one cannot assume that singing hymns and saying prayers constitutes religious education. It might constitute religious worship or religious activity, but it is not in parallel with any understanding we have of what education or religious education are.

Assembly is traditionally linked with RE, but collective worship (or, in some cases, secular moralising) is not the same as Religious Education.

Planning a year's RE: suggested steps

1. *At school level:* Has the school a policy for RE? Has the school devised a syllabus and schemes of work for RE in line with the agreed syllabus? Is there a designated teacher as co-ordinator for RE? Is the school providing adequate resources for the subject?

2. *At class level:* Identify the main general class topics for the year (not specifically RE). They will usually come from a school topic bank, perhaps complete with mapping and notes on non-RE ATs, devised to meet National Curriculum requirements and avoid overlap between classes.

3. Decide whether any of these topics allow a genuine rather than a forced religious education dimension and identify the dimension(s).

4. Relate the topics that allow for an RE dimension to RE ATs if in use in your school or LEA.

5. Select RE-led topics as well to build in to the emerging plan. These may be shorter than your large half-term topics from the school bank. Chapter 4 contains eight examples of RE-led 'mini-topics'. In a year it should be possible to include at least four RE-led topics or mini-topics in addition to the inevitable Christmas and Easter (and possibly harvest). A total of six, including Christmas and Easter, conveniently leads to one RE-led topic per half term.

6. In fleshing out the planning, consider how far the requirements of different pupil needs and abilities have been addressed and what methods for assessing, recording and reporting RE are to be employed. Have the faith backgrounds of children in the school been represented in the selection of topics?

7. Check whether the RE content you have now identified meets ATs in other areas. If so, it will be doubly valuable!

8. Start your detailed planning, with a confident smile. You have written some balanced RE on to your curriculum map for the year, so in your class at least it won't be an amateur hit-and-miss arrangement, and you will be laying the vital foundations for others to build on in subsequent RE!

IDEAS FOR INFANT RE

It should be emphasized that these ideas are intended as approaches and not detailed lesson plans. They aim to demonstrate possibilities across a variety of faith contexts of doing something with infants that really is RE rather than PSE or something else. Non-specialist infant teachers can turn them into material for their classes, using their general infant expertise and their specific knowledge of that particular group of children. For that reason we have tried to be flexible and to say 'or ... or ... or' where possible. That does not prevent the teacher turning them into 'and ... and ... and' if desired! Similarly, **Starting points** are intended as possible ways into a topic, or links with work that

may be in hand in other areas of the curriculum. They are not intended to be limiting by implying that there are no other ways into a topic; they are simply possible but not inevitable ways into the RE work.

Some topics will rightly be RE-led, even at infant level. Other work will be part of a wider or an integrated topic. In case studies from such topics – the last four in this chapter – sections in the text entitled **Starting points** and **Follow-up** may be dictated from the wider topic and may not be RE-specific. Also in integrated topics we have restricted the background notes for the teacher to RE aspects of the topic. An introduction to hydro-electric power for Year 1 does not appear here!

RE and Art

The great religions of the world have long used beautiful art and symbolism. Even Islam, perhaps the faith most reluctant to go in for pictures for religious reasons, has developed stunning calligraphy and symmetrical patterns. Art is one natural expression of faith, and art work is one natural way of developing or recording RE work in Key Stage 1.

The non-statutory guidance for Art in KS1 indicates that among the strands in AT1 (Investigating and Making) are the recording of 'what has been seen, imagined or remembered: visual perception; gathering and using resources and materials; using different materials and techniques in practical work and reviewing and modifying work'(B2). All these can be achieved through RE content. The more difficult Art AT for Key Stage 1, AT2 (Knowledge and Understanding), can also be reached via certain sorts of RE content. One way of 'recognising different kinds of art and their purposes'(B3) is to look at simple forms of art or symbols in different faiths during the RE work. Infants can then 'begin to make connections between their own work and that of other artists'(B3) by comparing suitable displays of their own work and material from the faith or story they have been illustrating (pictures in books, religious artefacts, etc.).

Many of the criteria for success in Key Stage 1 Art can be achieved through RE material (G1). Examples chosen from this book may well be more accessible to infants than some of the examples on page 5 of the statutory section of the Art document. Because this book is for teachers in RE, we thought it unnecessary to include detailed references to the Art document and its delivery, since the same could be done for several other subjects. But we do think these links matter and in the sort of planning envisaged in Chapter 3 teachers will wish to relate some of the practical RE examples here to ATs in Art and other curriculum fields.

NOAH (Jewish, Christian, Muslim)

Why do it?

- Some children have heard it already, have ark toys or know ark songs. They may grow up with literalist 'believe it or not' dilemmas about the history of Noah which miss the religious point of the story.

- Properly done, it avoids unhelpful ideas about God.

- It's a major story for these three faiths.

- Strands of the story are relevant to the children's experience.

BACKGROUND

This is an ancient narrative, which exists outside the Bible and the Qur'an in more ancient cultures that have disappeared, so it can be said to be one of the oldest stories in the world. Don't rely on your own childhood memories of this story. Read Genesis 6:9 to 9:17 which tells the best-known version of the story, though even this account combines two older sources, which the writer has hinted at by leaving discrepancies in the account (see, for example, 6:19 and 20 and 7:2).

There are three key ideas in the story: covenant (agreement), salvation and promise. The Qur'an emphasizes the theme of trust – Prophet Nuh's (Noah's) trust in Allah's promise – and adds the detail that there was a faithless son of Noah who refused to enter the ark and drifted away on the swirling waters (Sura 11). In Hebrew, the word 'ark' means a box, so we ought to picture the ark rather differently from the way in which it has traditionally been shown. Perhaps Noah released the raven and the dove by raising the lid from the inside!

Wiping out the world is not central to the story and we ought not, in fairness to all the three faiths that use it, picture God as an angry dictator snuffing out mankind. The story hinges on the three ideas mentioned above more than on punishment. In some ways the story of Jonah is a foil to this story (see p.20) because its counter proposal is one of forgiveness to the repentant world instead of destruction.

Starting points

Work on new starts, for example, or on promises or 'green' topics or rainbow and weather work.

Try

Tell the story, emphasizing the promise or the idea of agreement or trust. A picture of a rainbow can be used.

Then

Younger children might act out the story using a box on the water tray – one group at a time! Discuss with the class new starts they have experienced. For example, feelings about first going to school, moving to a new house, starting a new writing book at school (pages all fresh and clean), joining a new group, and so on. Record some of this in pictures or writing. The idea that forgiveness offers a new start could then be developed. Forgiveness can repair friendships. It can be part of a cycle: doing wrong or upsetting someone, being sorry, being forgiven, a new start. Can the children remember being and saying sorry about something? **What happened then? Is it always easy?** It will help them to understand that to the three faiths that tell this story, God is a forgiving God.

or

Discuss the idea of an agreement. (For example, '**If you keep your room tidy I'll give you ...**' '**I'll play with the best toy first, then we'll swap.**') Are promises easy to keep? Has God kept the promises in the story? Do we keep promises? Religious people believe that God always keeps promises.

or

Write and/or draw a saving story: a boat on the lake; washing blown off a line; a person at sea (this prepares for Jonah later); conservation – saving animals (the inevitable barn owls, dolphins and whales!). A poster could be made. Discuss: **How would you feel if one of your favourite animals became extinct? Draw an animal you feel it is very important to save.**

or

Hinduism provides the story of Manu's ark. **Manu, the first man, stood in water on one leg in prayer for many years. One day a small fish nudged his ankle. He put it in a bucket. But it grew and grew, so he put it in the river. Here it grew and grew until it blocked the river, so with great difficulty, because it was so big, he put it in the ocean to rescue it. Here it still grew but it had enough water to be free and safe. In return for its life being saved, the fish warned Manu of a flood that would cover the world, after which Brahma (God) would start again. So Manu collected the seed of every living thing and put them in a big boat. When the floods came, the giant fish towed Manu in his boat and looked after them all until the waters went back and the earth could be restocked with living creatures.** This story is told in more detail in *Stories from the Hindu World* (see Further Reading, p.59).

Follow-up

The story of Jonah (RE). The children could design a box/ark and consider the problems posed by keeping a lot of animals on a boat for a long time. How could these problems be solved? Floating and stability could be looked at: what sort of materials are waterproof, etc.? (Technology). In Maths, a two by two times table could be introduced, using pictures.

Noah took in:							made
1 set of 2	🐱🐱						2
2 sets of 2	🐱🐱	〰〰					4
3 sets of 2	🐱🐱	〰〰	🦆				6
4 sets of 2	🐱🐱	〰〰	🦆	🐌			8
5 sets of 2	🐱🐱	〰〰	🦆	🐌	🐷🐷		10
6 sets of 2	🐱🐱	〰〰	🦆	🐌	🐷🐷	🐭	12

The story of Noah can lead to an interesting Maths activity.

Children's views of the RE theme

JONAH (Jewish, Christian, Muslim)

Why do it?

● Some children know the story, but they may have problems with the science of it: how can a person survive inside a big fish? That could make them miss the religious point.

● It illustrates that truth can be conveyed through story.

● It was, in its day, controversial material: it showed God taking an interest in other nations (and faiths) and forgiving them.

● It's an important story for these three faiths.

BACKGROUND

Jonah is viewed as a Jewish minor prophet, and appears as a prophet in Islam, under the name Yunus. The whole book is the set reading for the afternoon service in synagogues on Yom Kippur, the Jewish Day of Atonement. Jesus made several references to the Jonah story and Christian tradition has been fascinated by the big fish, which has turned into a whale in the telling. Read the original story. The Book of Jonah contains a lot more events in the story than the popular retellings give us. In the Bible it appears towards the end of the Old Testament. In the Qur'an it is told more briefly in Sura 37:140 onwards.

It falls into three clear sections: Jonah's instructions, disobedience and punishment (1:1–16); his deliverance from the sea (1:17 – 2:10); and his preaching in Nineveh and its repentance. The backcloth is authentic: Joppa was a thriving port, Nineveh a once great capital city whose walls were 8 miles round. The Assyrian Empire around the River Tigris was real; it fell to the Chaldean-Babylonian Empire in 612 BCE. The British Museum Assyrian section gives some impression of the architecture and beliefs of this now extinct empire, which on various occasions invaded and severely mauled Israel. The book of Jonah teaches a controversial theme for some believers now: the universality of God's concern and care. Key words that could be explored are: forgive, sorry, warning, save or salvation.

Starting points

Work on storms or a monster/dinosaur project or work on journeys or the sea.

Try

Tell the story in instalments over three sessions, breaking at the points referred to above. Pictures of small boats – even modern ones – will help convey the atmosphere of being in a violent storm at sea in so small a vessel.

Then

Let groups of twos or threes use water play to act out the storm at sea part of the story.

or

Make pictures or collages of storms.

or

Discuss: **How do you feel when you've been given something really difficult to do? Is running away from things always/ever the answer? How do you feel when something you're very fond of gets broken or lost? In the story, how do you think God felt about Jonah running away (and about him sulking)?**

Follow-up

Read *The Dogger Story* (Picture Puffin) or try 'Doing Sorry' (for example, if a child has damaged someone's picture, they say sorry and help them to do another). As a class, you could write a story about hiding. Try 'Hard Targets' – everyone thinks of something they find hard to do at home or school and tries to do it (e.g. sharing toys, tidying a bedroom, learning a times table, getting up when the alarm goes, not moaning about helping with jobs at home). Record these on Hard Target sheets that can be displayed as a class record to see whether the targets can be reached.

Or ... link with work on signs

Discuss warning signs: labels about poisons; red flags; don't run in the corridors; don't smoke; don't get into cars with strangers; don't run on to the road. Play consequences with warnings: if you do this ... that might happen. If the children had to make some signs to put up in school, what would they choose? Make signs for some of their ideas. **What sign would we make to give to Jonah?**

Class 2H Things we find difficult	We did this on:				
	Monday	Tuesday	Wednesday	Thursday	Friday
Keeping the reading corner tidy	✓	✗	✗	✓	✓
Hanging our coats on pegs	✗	✓	✓	✗	✗
Remembering to put names on work	✗	✗	✓	✗	✓
Sitting quietly when Miss Jones comes in	✓	✗	✗	✓	✓

John Smith Things I find difficult	did this on:		(date)		
Remembering my reading folder	9th May	10th May	11th May	12th May	13th May
Remembering my PE kit	10th May	17th May			
Sharing the railway at school	12th May	15th May	17th May		
Remembering to give Mum school letters	10th May	18th May			

Hard Target sheets can be used to record both individual and collective goals.

EASTER (Christian, pre-Christian)

Why do it?

● Easter is the major Christian festival.

● Pre-Christian spring rituals survive.

● The Easter holiday, with chocolate eggs and so on, has become part of the secular culture and therefore the experience of most children in Britain.

BACKGROUND

For Christians Easter celebrates the resurrection of Jesus, and while they may differ in their interpretation of this event, they agree that it forms the central point of the Christian faith. The belief is that Jesus is still in some sense alive; he didn't raise himself – God did it. After his execution (provable history) his disciples experienced his presence in some form, according to the gospels in visible appearances. Earlier evidence is in I Corinthians 15, written in 50 CE, fifteen years before the earliest surviving gospel, Mark. Christians claim that Jesus is present with them now and especially when they worship together.

The name 'Easter' comes from a pre-Christian Germanic goddess, Ostera or Eostre, whose festival marked the arrival of spring. Pre-Christian customs for springtime survive. Among them are: the well-dressings in Derbyshire which were later Christianised; Ashbourne shrovetide football match, which may once have been played with a human head as the ball; Flora Day in Helston and the Obby Oss in Padstow. These and many other local customs celebrate the arrival of spring. Key words to explore: life, joy, new.

Starting points

Through spring topics; through the approach of Eastertide itself.

Try

Find out what the children already know about Easter. If possible, make a small display that includes a hot cross bun, a crucifix and a religious Easter card. Question the children about the items. Do

A display of some of the symbols associated with Easter will provide an introduction to this most important of Christian festivals.

they know what they are and what they remind us of? This will lead on to the basic story. Start by telling them that Jesus was killed (no need for gruesome detail). Older infants can follow that this was because people didn't understand what he was trying to tell them and they were angry at some of the things he said.

Even his friends left him. But three days later these friends changed from being upset and sad to very happy. They said they'd seen Jesus again, that he was alive. He didn't look exactly as he did before, but now he was going to live for ever. Christians believe that although they can't see Jesus as his friends said they could, they can still talk to him. That's why Easter is the best day of the year for them. On Easter eve some churches are completely dark and then one big Easter candle is lit to remind people of Jesus, and from that candle are lit all the little candles that everyone is holding, until the whole church is light.

Then

On a separate occasion talk about spring festival customs and the fact that Easter eggs and pictures of baby animals represent new life. Older infants can understand aspects of spring rituals. For useful material see Further Reading, p.59.

Follow-up

With your class, make an Easter garden. This is a miniature garden made in a small tray. Use soil, stones, small plants and anything you can think of for the garden. Make a cave out of stones, with the entrance open to view and the inside empty to represent the empty tomb.

Alternatively, do a class drama or assembly about Jesus's friends. Start with twelve children plus one. As you tell the story, twelve leave one on his own. Then one goes and twelve are sad. Then one returns, and gradually more and more are added until the whole class is at the front, representing the growth of Christianity. (This may be an unsuitable option in some multifaith classes.)

or

Try out some of the customs based on eggs, e.g. dyeing, painting, rolling down banks (hard boil them first!). Make Easter cards and baskets. Produce a class booklet entitled 'New Life at Easter', with pictures of trees blossoming, birds returning after the winter, chickens, lambs, etc. (include also Christians being happy about Jesus's return). Or perhaps each child could produce an individual short booklet. Another idea would be to make a large collage.

The ancient custom of well-dressing dates back to pagan times, though it has since become Christianised. The dressing is made entirely of flower petals and other natural objects.

CHRISTMAS (pre-Christian, Christian, secular)

Why do it?

● It's unavoidable, from September onwards!

BACKGROUND

For more than 300 years, the Christian Church did not celebrate Jesus's birth. The main festival was – and still is – Easter. But when Christianity became the official religion of the Roman Empire, Jesus was awarded an official birthday, and an attempt to clean up the excesses of the Roman feast of Saturnalia (17 December onwards) began.

Cards are a recent addition, dating only from Victorian times. Token presents only were exchanged until after the Second World War. The pre-Christmas season of Advent was strictly kept – there were no decorations until Christmas Eve, and no carols except Advent carols were sung before Christmas day. Christmas carols filled the twelve days of Christmas. Epiphany (January 6) celebrates the wise men bringing their gifts, for the church calendar, like the Bible, sees their visit as separate from that of the shepherds.

So the modern Christmas in Britain is a mixture of pre-Christian winter festival (the eating and drinking), Jesus's official birthday, later Christian legend, and a secular and very materialistic long winter holiday for the fortunate western world. Today there is the beginning of a radical movement to get back to a simpler Christmas. How many teachers would agree!

It is vital for the teacher to read the gospel stories for herself. There is no snow, the number of wise men (not kings) is unknown, the shepherds do not bring lambs and in one account Jesus is born at home! The Qur'an has Jesus born in a remote place by a palm tree when the dates were ripe – an interestingly different setting for this year's nativity play perhaps! The gospel accounts are in Matthew 1:18 to 2:23 and Luke 2:1–21. The Qur'an refers to Jesus's birth in Sura 19:23 and in 3:46 onwards.

Starting points

Keep the start of work on Christmas as late as you can in the autumn term, otherwise children and staff 'peak' too early. Discussion can begin with what the children already know about Christmas and the things that are happening all around them – decorations in shops, Christmas lights and so on. Discussing what the festival is about can promote useful PSE: many youngsters are in the 'I want ... I want ... ' mode.

Try

Tell the story in three sessions: (1) the journey and birth; (2) the shepherds; (3) the wise men.

Then

For the first part of the story (1), try any of the following. Compare a modern birth with Jesus's birth. **How do you think Mary felt about the long journey? What does the mother need to prepare for going to hospital and for a new baby? What did Jesus's mother do? There was no hospital then. Journeys are often nice, but this one was not.** Discuss why (accommodation, late stages of pregnancy). *Or* develop the 'not wanted' theme. **How do you feel when people don't want you to play? How do you think Mary felt when they couldn't get in at the inn?** *Or* develop the new baby theme. Perhaps 'borrow' a mum with a new baby. **How did Mary feel about her new baby? How do people usually feel about new babies?** ('Miss, my Daddy said, "Oh God,

Christmas provides opportunities for practical work, such as making decorations, but the focus needs to be on the story of Jesus's birth and its significance for Christians.

not another...".') You could display photographs of the class and 'Miss' as babies. This can lead on to discussion about what the children can do now that they couldn't do as babies. **Why were there no photographs of Jesus?** 'They were too poor to have a camera ...'

For (2), face the 'angels' issue. **Angels are messengers.** (That's what the word means in Greek and Hebrew.) **Because Christmas cards show them with wings doesn't mean they *are* like that. Do you think the shepherds really saw and heard them in their heads? Were the angels really there in the field? What do you think? This baby was very important, but ordinary (or 'unimportant') people saw him first.**

For (3), concentrate on the words 'king' and 'giving'. **The wise men were expecting an important person to be born. They had heard of a king, so they went to see the King (Herod) to ask about it. Herod thought that *he* was the important person and he wanted no other king around, so he told them to go and find this supposed king. They found Jesus. He didn't look important and he wasn't born where you'd expect a king to be born, but they accepted that he was a king and they gave him suitable presents. Because they did not like King Herod they went home another way.**

Follow-up

Teachers will need fewer suggestions here than anywhere, for they will probably be used to making cards, calendars and little presents. Look for a new angle in discussion as the children are busy with all these things. **Presents are not always things. You could dry the dishes as a present. To parents, a baby can be a present. To Christians, Jesus is a 'present' from God. He wouldn't have had lots of toys or expensive presents, but he would have had presents 'with love'. Does the label showing love matter more than the thing? 'Yes, miss.' 'Shall I ask all your mums and dads to give you labels instead of presents this Christmas?'**

An alternative would be to let each child make a book – or make a class book together – of the Christmas story or a part of it.

Did you enjoy reading and doing this book?

Did you try hard?

Teacher comment

Name ....

Why do we celebrate Christmas?

How did you feel at Christmas time?

Did you share your Christmas presents with anyone?

AGNI, *the hidden fire (Hinduism)*

Why do it?

- It's a well-known Hindu story about a popular god.

- Some people see in it themes that are common to other cultures as well as Hindu. It deals with fear, threat, comfort and trust.

BACKGROUND

A version of the story, written for young children, can be found in *Stories from the Hindu World* (see Further Reading, p.59). The following is a summary of the story.

The gods were looking everywhere for Lord Agni. He was the god of fire – of the fire in the sun as well as fires in people's homes. The bad gods were afraid of him, which is why the good gods wanted to find him. He hid underwater, but he made the water hot and a small frog told the gods where he was hiding. This made Agni very angry and he told the little frog that in future he would have no tongue, then he couldn't tell on people! Agni ran off and hid again, so that when the other gods arrived they found only the little frog crying. They tried to comfort him and told him that he could make different noises and that the earth, which is alive, would always look after him.

Agni had gone to hide in a fig tree, but his heat and light burnt its leaves and an elephant told the gods where he was hiding. This made Agni very angry again and he told the elephant that from now on his tongue would only bend backwards. The gods arrived too late again, but they comforted the elephant by telling him that from now on he would make a sound as fine and glorious as a trumpet. The elephant was pleased about that.

Agni was now hiding inside a hollow tree. This time it was a parrot who told the gods where he was. Agni yelled at the parrot and told him he would never speak again. This time the gods caught up with Agni. But first they comforted the parrot by telling him that from now on he would make the sound small children make – 'Ka!'. So the parrot was happy.

As Agni, the fire, roared out of the top of the hollow tree angrily, the gods asked him why he kept running away when they needed his help. Agni reminded them that they had used his fire brothers and when they had finished with them they had blown them out, so that was the end of them! 'Will you do that to me?' he asked, frightened. But the gods promised Agni that he should have the sami tree as his home and that when anyone rubbed two of its sticks together they would remake the god's fire. Agni was very happy. He could trust the gods and the gods could trust him. He became a messenger for the gods from then on and made fire even in the poorest homes to keep the people warm. He gave people light in the darkness and warmth in the cold.

Starting points

Work on heat, light or the planets.

Try

Show the children pictures of the story (see the version referred to above) or use pictures of the animals involved as you tell the story.

Then

Discuss: **Agni hid because he was afraid. Have you ever felt afraid? When? Being afraid made him angry with the animals** who'd told where he was. Being afraid or lonely can sometimes make people cross or unfriendly. Should we help new children in the school, or children who are left out of others' games? When we meet somebody new, what do we do to welcome them? What sort of people shouldn't we trust? (Strangers who offer sweets, etc.)

or

Discuss: **Can you think of any times when you were afraid of something (such as first day at school) that turned out to be all right? If it's something in the near future record first what you think it might be like and then later what it *was* like.**

or

Ask the children to write an 'afraid' story that has a happy ending.

or

Discuss: **The gods in the story comforted the animals and made them feel better. Who has done this for you? When? How? Have you ever done it for someone else? When? What did you do? Sometimes things as well as people can do this: for example, teddy bears in bed, lights on when it's dark,** warmth when you're cold. Draw a picture of a time when someone or something made you feel better (perhaps a hug or cuddle with mum, dad or friends?) and caption it. Who would the animals like best – the god who was cross with them or the gods who comforted them? Many religious people believe that they can trust God to look after them however bad things seem to be, sometimes even when they can't see a happy ending ahead.**

or

Discuss: **This story began in the east many years ago. Fire was important for light and heat, and people had to be able to make fires to live. What do you think the story said to them?** Compare lighting and heating that the children have encountered.

or

Discuss: **Think of a time when you've felt angry. What was it about? What did you want to do? What *did* you do? What could you have done instead? If you had to choose a colour for anger, what would you choose? And for warmth? And for fire? Talk about your choices. Use them in a picture of something in this story.**

Agni is the Hindu god of fire. His story contains themes of fear, comfort and trust.

DIVALI (Hinduism, Sikhism)

Why do it?

● This festival is important for both faiths.

● Although the stories told differ in each faith, the theme is the triumph of good over evil and light over darkness, a theme which extends beyond the two faiths that celebrate this festival.

BACKGROUND

Hinduism

The festival is marked by the lighting of lamps (divas) to represent (a) the story of the return of the good king Rama to his kingdom, or (b) the yearly coming of Lakshmi, goddess of wealth – hence bills are paid and financial plans made for the year ahead. The Lakshmi story related here can be found in *Stories from the Hindu World* (see Further Reading, p.59). This is a summary.

An Indian queen used to ask her husband for very expensive Divali presents every year. One year she asked for expensive and very rare pearls in a necklace. He agreed and obtained them for her. Next morning when she went down to the river to bathe she lay the necklace on top of her pile of clothes, but a crow swooped down and carried the necklace away, dropping it on the doorstep of a poor woman's hut. The woman shared the hut with a friend called Poverty and they had been together for years.

The queen was so upset and sulky about the loss of the necklace that the king ordered a search through the whole country. A reward was offered. But the old poor woman put the necklace on and went straight to the palace to hand it in. The king and queen were delighted and prepared to give her the reward money, but to their surprise she refused it and asked a favour instead. This was that the king should order that no Divali lamps be lit except in the poor woman's house for that particular year. He did this, and as night fell, the poor woman's hut was the only place in the land to be lit up.

Lakshmi, going from house to house to bring wealth, was lost. She could see no lights to welcome her, except in one place, the hut, so she hurried to the hut gladly and knocked at the door, pleading to be let in. The poor woman agreed, on condition that Lakshmi should stay with her for seven generations. At this, Poverty pleaded to be let out, as there wasn't room for both her and Lakshmi in the hut. She promised not to return for seven generations. So they all lived happily!

Sikhism

Guru Nanak, the founder of Sikhism, had been brought up as a Hindu and the new faith continued to celebrate Divali. But later Sikhs told a different Divali story, one relating to their guru, Guru Hargobind (1595–1644 CE). This is a summary.

Guru Hargobind became a guru at the age of eleven, after the martyrdom of his father. He wore two swords instead of the one previously worn. He was imprisoned by Emperor Jehangir because of his father's unpaid debts.

Jehangir looked into Hargobind's case and ordered his release from prison. But in the prison with him were fifty-two Indian princes. Hargobind said that he wouldn't leave unless they too could be released. Jehangir did not wish to release them, but as a concession agreed that as many as could hold on to Hargobind's cloak as he went along the very narrow exit passage could go free. Hargobind produced a coat with long tassels attached, so that all the fifty-two princes were able to hold it and went free.

Like Hindus, Sikhs mark Divali with lights, fireworks and presents.

At the festival of Divali rows of lamps are lit. In this Hindu temple people are offering gifts of flowers, fruit and money to the goddess Lakshmi.

Starting points

Work on light. Another possibility is work on honesty/integrity.

Try

Tell one story, or both (but on different occasions).

Then

Make a class picture-book or mural of the story. *Or* (for Lakshmi) discuss: **Things I wouldn't like to lose; precious or special things I would want to get back. What makes them precious – their cost or their value as gifts, if they were given? What do they look like?** Children could record them individually or make a class book: 'Class 2's Special Things'.

or

Discuss the key word 'lost'. **Lakshmi was lost. Have you ever been lost? How did it feel? Write a story about it, or make up a story about being lost. (You could be the person who was lost.)** Then tell the children Jesus's stories about lost things: sheep (Luke 15:1–7); a coin (Luke 15:8–10); a person (Luke 15:11–32). In both the Lakshmi and the Luke material it is possible to lead on to the idea of being found. **How would the person feel? How might you feel?**

or

Obtain a diva for the children to see and then perhaps make a simple one. (If you have Hindu or Sikh children in the class, they may be able to bring some in.)

or

Act out one of the stories.

or

Discuss the Hargobind story and develop the idea of unselfishness and sharing. **Hargobind could have walked out free and left the others behind. He chose not to. Why? Is it hard to share? What do we share? What do you think the princes felt when they were out of prison? How do you think the emperor felt when he heard about it? Do you think they said 'Thank you' to Hargobind? Do people say 'Thank you' on 'Jim'll fix it'?** Read the children *The Elephant and the Bad Baby* by Elfrida Vipont and Raymond Briggs (Puffin).

This material does not perhaps have an obviously religious follow-up, except in the story of Jesus and the ten lepers (Luke 17:11–19). It is nevertheless religious material, because it is part of a wider religious tradition. Lakshmi remains a god in Hinduism, Hargobind remains a guru – one of God's chosen spokesmen – in Sikhism, both elements that should not be edited out in the telling.

PROPHET MUHAMMAD AND THE SPIDER

(Muslim)

Why do it?

● It's a story from the life of the Prophet that small children can understand and sympathise with.

● It makes the point that even creatures we may find unappealing can be vital to our survival.

BACKGROUND

The story comes from the Prophet's famous journey from Makkah to Madinah, the journey known to Muslims as the Hijirah (622 CE), from which the Muslim calendar – AH (after Hijirah) – begins. It is told in *The Life of Muhammad* (see Further Reading, p.59). Prophet Muhammad (the preferred spelling to Mohammed), to Muslims the Seal of the Prophets, is greatly respected in Islam, but not worshipped. He is not God (Allah), nor is he God's son. To Muslims he is the last and greatest of the prophets, who began with Adam and included Jesus. In order to avoid a *faux pas* with Muslim children in your class, it is important to know that it is not considered respectful to draw the Prophet's face in Islamic art. If he is shown at all it is from behind. The essence of this story is as follows:

Muhammad was fleeing from his enemies from Makkah (preferred spelling to Mecca). They were pursuing him because he was opposed to the worship of numerous gods there. Armed men came to his house to kill him as he slept, but they found his cousin Ali sleeping under Muhammad's cloak instead. Meanwhile Muhammad escaped by camel to the mountains. A reward of one hundred camels, a very great deal, was offered for his capture.

Muhammad and his friend Abu Bakr hid in a cave, living on sheep's milk and food brought by another friend, Abd Allah and his sister Asma. A spider started to spin its web across the cave mouth and doves built a nest on the floor near the entrance.

When the Makkans arrived they thought that the Prophet might be hiding in the cave, but the flying up of the dove from its nest and the extensive spider's web convinced them that the cave must have been empty for years, so they didn't bother to enter and search it. In this way Muslims believe God kept the Prophet safe.

Starting points

Work on ecology or the inter-dependence of species, both less off-putting than they sound in the infant classroom!

Try

Tell the story.

Then

Find out about spiders: number of legs, eyes, what they eat, how many different kinds there are.

or

Discuss the key word 'friend'. **Muhammad couldn't have managed without friends. Who were they? They were Abu Bakr, Abd Allah, Asma and the spider and the dove. Tell us about a friend who's helped you and a time when you helped a friend. We have animals as friends. What do we call them? What's the difference between them and other animals? Was the spider a pet?**

or

Discuss the key words 'save' and 'safe'.

Muslims believe that Allah (God) kept Muhammad safe. **What do you think? Do you think God looks after people? Who looks after you?** (You could refer to the Noah and Jonah stories above.) **Sometimes we can keep ourselves safe.** (Discuss rules for the classroom, playground, home, kitchen and road safety.) **Sometimes we can't manage on our own, we need other people like the lollipop lady, mums and dads, and, for religious people, God.**

or

Produce a class collage of the cave scene (not showing Muhammad). Include the dove on its nest, the spider spinning its web, and perhaps Muhammad's friends or his enemies searching for him.

When Muhammad hid in a cave to evade his enemies, his presence was concealed by a spider's web and a dove's nest.

SIDDHARTHA'S STORY (Buddhism)

Why do it?

- Siddhartha (the Buddha) is one of the most influential religious figures in the world.

- There are contact points in the story with the lives of children: for example, being spoilt or protected, reacting to cruelty to animals, meeting death for the first time, the value of quiet times.

BACKGROUND

The Buddha (like the Christ) is a title, meaning 'the awakened one'. The life of the Buddha can be pieced together only from passing references in the three Pitaka (baskets), the basic 'scriptures'. This is a summary of the story, one version of which can be found in *The Life of the Buddha* (see Further Reading, p.59).

Siddhartha's mother had a dream that an elephant entered her right side Some time afterwards Siddhartha was born – painlessly out of his mother's right side, according to legend – the son of the ruler of a small kingdom in north-east India (563 BCE).

The king, afraid that his son might leave to become a holy man, provided him with toys, games, gardens, sports training, and three palaces. But he was not to leave the palace grounds. One day when Siddhartha was in the palace gardens, a wounded swan fell at his feet. It had been shot by a bow and arrow. Siddhartha started to nurse the swan, but he was interrupted by the arrival of his cousin, Devadatta, who had shot it and claimed it as his. This led to a quarrel as to whose swan it was, and they decided to go to a holy man. He ruled that as it is better to save life than to destroy it, the swan belonged to Siddhartha. When it was better, it was allowed to go free.

At the age of sixteen Siddhartha married the beautiful princess Yasodhara and they had a son, Rahula. But Siddhartha wanted to see life outside the palace walls and so he went out on three successive days. On the first day he saw Decay (old age) – he had never before seen an old, wasted body. On the second day he saw Disease – he had never been allowed to see sickness before. On the third day he saw Death – a dead body being carried away for cremation – for the first time. He began to wonder why people had to hurt, to be sad and unhappy.

He decided to leave the palace in the middle of the night to try living the life of a holy man. He gave away his jewels and his rich clothes and lived a very hard life, sleeping outdoors, starving himself, but finding no answer to the sadness in the world. So he left the holy men and went to sit quietly under the bodhi tree. There he became aware of the answer: if we see something nice we want it and if we see something horrible we push it away. That's why we're never content, never really happy. He found a place inside himself away from all this, a place of deep peace. Buddhists call it 'Nirvana'.

Starting points

Quiet times in class, perhaps after a noisy day when the teacher has kept asking for quiet, or the delightful and rare times when a class is naturally occupied and quiet. Work about 'our town/village'.

Try

Tell the story, in instalments if necessary, being sensitive to children who have experienced death (perhaps a grandparent or other relative, or a pet).

Then

Make a frieze of the story. Discuss: **Do you think it is better to save things or kill them? Who do you think should have had the swan? Why?** (Not all the children will agree.)

or

Key word: 'old'. **Do you think people who are old are always unhappy? Do you know anyone who is old? What can you do because you're young that they can't do? What happens to someone's body when they are old?** Ask the children if possible to bring in photographs of their grandparents, and perhaps also photos of them when they were young.

or

Key word: 'unhappy'. **Can you tell us about some things that have made you unhappy?**

Could anything have made them better? Record them in writing or drawing.

or

Key word: 'quiet'. **Do you ever like to be quiet? Where can you go to be quiet? What do you do then? Do you take anything with you?** Get the children to be quiet for a time. **What can you hear in the silence? If you close your eyes, what can you see in your head that makes you feel peaceful? Draw it. What colours make you feel like that? If you're in a temper, do you try going off to be quiet somewhere? What happens to your temper?**

or

Key word: 'death'. **Have you had a pet that died? Did you see the pet after it was dead? Did it look different? How? Did it look peaceful? What did you do with it? What happens then? How did you feel? Why? Did you cry? Did that make you feel better? In peace and quiet, the Buddha lost some of his sadness.**

Statues of the Buddha, like this one in Thailand, usually show him attaining enlightenment.

HAPPINESS (any faith, or humanist theme)

Why do it?

● It helps children to come to terms with their experiences and feelings.

● It helps children to be sensitive to feelings in others.

● It demonstrates that, for believers, religion can be the key to happiness.

BACKGROUND

A rosary is a special string of beads, available quite cheaply from shops stocking Roman Catholic and Anglican prayer books and aids to devotion. It is used by many Roman Catholics, and by some Anglicans, when they pray. The rosary is an aid to memory. The person praying 'tells' the beads, that is they recite prayers as they work round the beads. There are three parts to telling a rosary (Joyful, Sorrowful and Glorious), each containing a set of five of the fifteen 'mysteries' or deep religious truths. For children these can be called Happy, Sad and Special.

On the rosary each of the five subdivisions contains ten Hail Marys, an Our Father and usually a Gloria – all set prayers that can be recited from memory. The Birmingham RISC Project (see p.59) offers an alternative use of these beads in early years RE, set in the context of the story of Bernadette and Our Lady of Lourdes. They retain the use of the words Joyful, Sorrowful and Glorious.

Beads are used as aids to prayer in several faiths. In Hinduism, a mala is a string of 108 beads. The Hindu uses them while repeating the name of God to help achieve union with the Supreme. In Sikhism, the mala is made of knotted cotton and the Sikh repeats the words 'Wonderful Lord' as each knot is passed through the fingers.

In Islam a subha is a string of 100 beads, made of bone or wood or metal, used to remind the believer of the 100 names of Allah (God). There are three sets of thirty-three, and one isolated bead. Muslims hold each bead in turn between the thumb and forefinger, reciting each name of God in turn, and pausing to think about it. There must be no other speaking or interruptions during this activity, which is preceded by ritual cleansing. That accounts for the ninety-nine names of Allah. What about the isolated bead? The story goes that the greatest name, the hundredth, is hidden in the Qur'an. Only the camel knows what it is. He can't tell us and he doesn't know the other ninety-nine!

In all these faiths the use of the beads is optional; users find them helpful for developing concentration and devotion in their private prayer.

This Muslim woman is holding a subha, a string of 100 beads used to remind the believer of the names of God.

Starting points

The topic could be introduced in a variety of ways. It might arise spontaneously as part of other work on, for example, the child, the school, the family, new life (how we feel when we see a new baby or a baby animal), or discussion about the weather (how we feel when the sun shines).

Try

Oral work (or a worksheet, if preferred) on: **What do you like/dislike at school/home? When do you feel happy at school/home? How can you tell when someone is happy? What can we do to stop people being sad? How do we feel when our best friends/Mum/Dad are sad?** The responses may be simply recorded in pictures or writing.

or

Make a sad/happy paper. Fold a sheet of paper into either two or four parts and draw sad and happy pictures or facial expressions on each. *Or* make masks to show sad or happy expressions (pictures of the comedy and tragedy masks once used in theatres may be helpful). *Or* **paint a happy face – a friend or yourself (you will need to use a mirror).**

Then

Introduce a rosary: **these beads are used by some Christians to help them say prayers. When they hold a bead they say a prayer and then go on to the next bead. As they go round the loop of the beads they may think first of the happy times and then of the sad times for Jesus's mother. The last time round the loop is for the special or glorious times for her. Can you think of a really special time for her?** (If they don't suggest it, having Jesus as a baby was one of them!)

Introduce subha beads: **these beads are used by Muslims to remind them of God's names and as they say each one, they think carefully about it. It helps them to feel closer to Allah (God).** Tell the story of the camel.

Children can draw happy faces as part of a topic on happiness.

Then

Let the children record their own happy, sad and special times. This can be done by giving each child a piece of paper on which, using a template, they can draw three circles or 'beads' and record one occasion in each, with a picture and a few words of explanation. They can then draw a chain linking the beads. Alternatively, for class display or with younger children, each child can record one happy, sad or special occasion on a larger circle of paper or a paper plate; these can then be strung together to make the class's own happy, sad or special chains. Another option is to string pictures downwards to make mobiles, in sets of three – happy, sad and special.

or

Discuss: **How do we remind ourselves about things that are important? We put notices on the classroom wall. How does mum remind herself about shopping? Religious people sometimes wear or use special things to remind themselves about God. They use beads, crosses, crucifixes, turbans, badges, statues, pictures, bells, and so on.** Display some of these items in the classroom.

Follow-up

If possible, let the children see a mala and explain its use. You could use the FARE happy/sad self-assessment sheet for the work in this topic.

INTEGRATED TOPIC: Colour and light

Why do it?

● These things are very much within the child's experience.

● Different colours, and the symbolism of light, are significant for some of the world faiths.

BACKGROUND

Hinduism uses fire and light in its worship. For example, the festival of Holi is celebrated by bonfires. At the festival of Divali small lights are lit to help the goddess Lakshmi (Wealth) find her way into the home for the coming year and the story of Rama rescuing his wife Sita from the evil king Ravana is told, often in dance and drama.

In Buddhism the notion of enlightenment – a sort of light and sight – is central and children can be told a little about the enlightment of Siddhartha (the Buddha) under the bodhi tree (see p.34).

Judaism has the festival of Hanukah, when candles are lit for eight nights, a new one being added each night, with a ninth being used as the 'servant light' to light the others. It celebrates the rededication of the Jerusalem Temple and the legend or miracle of the Temple light whose oil did not run out for eight days (I Maccabees 4). Each Friday night, Shabbat (the sabbath) begins when candles are lit and prayers said for the special meal. Shabbat ends with a ceremony using a plaited havdalah candle to mark the return from rest to work.

In Christianity, Jesus is seen as the Light of the World; light is used especially in the Gospel of John as a symbol of goodness. Colours are used as symbols in Christian worship and can

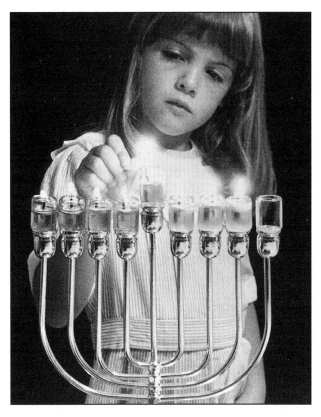

At the Jewish festival of Hanukah an eight-branched candlestick represents the miracle of the Temple lamp. This girl is using the servant light to light the others.

be seen in altar cloths, pulpit hangings or perhaps in what the priest wears: green (general); purple (penitence); white (festivals); red (Whitsun and martyrs).

Sikhism also has Divali, but the central story is different from the Hindu one: it is the story of Guru Hargobind's famous rescue of fifty-two Indian princes from captivity when he was released from prison (see p.30).

A note of historical warning. Joseph's 'many coloured coat', which seems so apt for this topic, was actually white. An early Bible translator – faced with an unknown word – guessed that the coat must have been many coloured, because at the time of the translation the rich wore such coats. But as the Hebrew language became better understood and translated, it was realised that the word the translator had guessed at in fact meant a long white garment with sleeves. Oh dear, the musical will have to be rewritten ...!

Starting points

This could arise from various topics: e.g. home, power, planets or light and lighting. Work on colour logically develops from light.

Try

Talk about different sources of light, natural and human-made. **Why is light important? What can you do with it?** Explain that light often stands for good, and dark for bad. **Why do you think this is? Candles are used in some churches and oil lamps in some temples because of this, not to replace electric lights but because they mean something.**

Then

Use story material from any of the faiths represented among the children (see the Background notes above).

or

Prepare a display of religious lights, including a baptism candle, a hanukah menorah (candelabra), a diva, a paschal candle, a havdalah candle, etc.

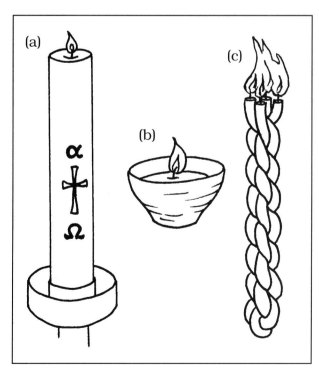

(a) Baptism candle (Christianity)   (b) Diva (Hinduism)
(c) Havdalah candle (Judaism)

or

Explore feelings about light and dark. Do the children feel worried or frightened in the dark? Do a worksheet: 'In the light I can ...' (clean my teeth, etc.), 'In the dark I can ...' This will reveal that one can do very little! They'll keep assuming light, for example, 'Watch TV' or 'Use a torch'. **What happens when we try to do things in the dark? We might fall or hurt ourselves. How do you feel in the bedroom with your light off? Or do you prefer to leave it on when you go to sleep?** Record feelings about the dark, perhaps in a poem.

or

Make candles *or* use a simple circuit to light a bulb.

or

Think about light in history. **What would it have been like to use candles? What happens when your lights go out at home?** Look at a simple wick lamp.

Then

Lead on to a discussion about colour. **We can see colours when we have light. In the English language, colours can be matched to our feelings, for example, red for anger, blue for cold, green for envy. Colours can be used in places of worship to show the sort of things we are thinking about on that occasion.** Discuss some of the colours and see if the children can see why they've been used.

Follow-up

Look at warm and cold colours. Ask the children to draw a warm pattern and a cold one. Discuss colour sayings, e.g. white as snow, or let the children invent some. **What's a good colour for angry?** Discuss colour changes, as in fruit ripening, leaves dying, and cakes browning. If the season is right, you could let some tomatoes ripen in the classroom; this can lead into Science work – and tasting!

CONCEPT CHART

The most colourful thing you know.

Where do we get light from?

Where is there darkness?

Favourite colours.

LIGHT AND COLOUR

People of the world.

Where do you see candles?

INTEGRATED TOPIC: Water

Why do it?

● For several world faiths, water is a powerful symbol of cleansing.

● Using water for washing and drinking, seaside holidays, learning to swim, water play at school, are all within the child's experience.

● There is an increasing environmental emphasis on water and its provision.

BACKGROUND

In the ancient world in which most major faiths grew, water was a rare commodity. In hot climates it gave relief; it was relaxing and soothing. It cleansed. Most of all it gave life, and droughts were greatly feared. The water-seller was an important person in many ancient cultures.

Hindu worship recognises the importance of water. It is one of the elements from which everything is made, represented on the special worship tray (called an arti) used in acts of worship. The other elements represented are earth (incense and flowers), fire (lights), air (the waving of a fan) and ether (a conch shell is blown during the ceremony to represent this). There are also sacred rivers in India. The Ganga Ma, mother Ganges, is often visited by pilgrims, who bathe in its waters. After cremation the ashes of the dead are scattered on a sacred river, preferably the Ganges, and those of Hindus not resident in India may be flown there for the ceremony to be performed.

Christianity uses water in one of its major sacraments, baptism. Here it is a symbol of cleansing and new life. In its more dramatic form – believer's baptism by total immersion in a river or baptistry tank – the water closing over the person also symbolises death (by drowning) and being raised to a new life in Christ.

In Islam, paradise is talked of as being a garden of delight, with groves of trees and cool waters – especially appealing in the desert countries of its origin. At least once a day, before the five cycles of prayer, Muslims must perform wudhu or wuzu, using pure running water to wash themselves in a fixed ritual manner: hands, mouth, face, right hand and arm to elbow, then left hand and arm, head and neck, ears, right foot as far as the ankle, then the left foot in the same way. The aim is to approach God pure in body as well as mind.

For Sikhs, washing is part of their preparation for entering the room in the temple in which their holy book, the Guru Granth Sahib, is present. Like their founder, Guru Nanak, Sikhs are expected to rise early, then wash and pray.

An arti tray is used in Hindu worship. It holds symbols of the elements water, earth and fire.

Starting points

A 'green' topic, or work on the rain cycle or on homes (water supplies).

Try

Discussion: How we get our water supplies. Why it's important. Its wider uses, such as irrigating crops and providing power. Consider other countries where water is neither clean nor easily found – use pictures and maps. **Water is also used in religions. In these, cleansing with water stands for being clean from the things we've done wrong. Some religious people use it just once, at a very special time when they make themselves clean and start again with God. Other religious people use water a lot, to prepare themselves for prayer.**

Then

How is water used in religions we know? (In a multi-faith class children will be able to give examples of some of the different religious practices listed above.)

or

Has anyone been to a baptism or a christening? (Someone may be able to talk about their experience.) **What happens? Can you bring any photographs in for us to look at? Did you know that some Christians baptise grown-ups? Why is this different?** (You have to make the decision yourself.) **Some churches have a special ceremony called confirmation where people who were baptised as babies can, if they choose, promise to carry on being Christians. To Christians, baptism is about coming into the church (joining it) and making a new start. When a baby is baptised, do you think it will never do anything wrong afterwards? What happens when we do something wrong? We look for a new start.**

or

Arrange for a local member of one of the faith communities to call in and conduct a brief interview with them. A vicar might be able to bring a portable font! (Many churches use them.)

or

Some Christians practise baptism by total immersion, sometimes – as here – in the 'living' water of a river. The water is a symbol of cleansing and new life.

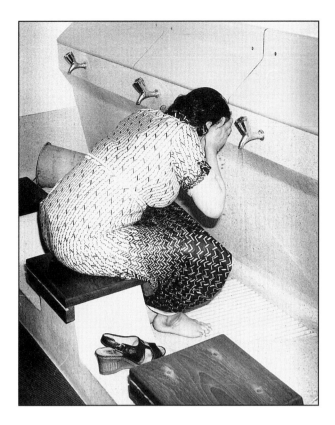

To Muslims water is also a symbol of cleansing. This woman is performing the ritual washing that precedes prayer in a mosque.

A pilgrim bathes in one of the sources of the Ganges, a sacred river of Hindusim.

In Islam and Sikhism, people use water to make themselves clean before doing something very important – saying prayers. We wash before a special occasion like a party and we put on clean, washed clothes when we go to see someone special. Record this by asking the children to do some 'getting ready' pictures (or writing): for example, having a bath before going on holiday, or making ourselves smart to go and see Grandma.

or

For Hindus, the Ganges is a very special river. People will go to a lot of trouble to bathe there. Some Hindus in other countries will travel all the way to India. Have you a special place or a special thing you want to do very much? Record this in a picture or writing.

or

In Islam, paradise is a beautiful place where you hope to go after you die. It's like a really beautiful garden where everyone will be happy. Why would a garden like that need water? For the plants, to make them flower in all sorts of colours. To keep the garden cool, perhaps. **For beauty, like a fountain or the sea. Do you like water on a very hot day, for a cool swim? Do you like a hot bath on a really cold day?**

(If you are visiting a place of worship as part of another RE topic, point out the facilities connected with water, for instance, the ablution area in a mosque.)

Follow-up

Develop further the idea of washing. **When we wash, what do we want to get rid of? We might have a choice of hot, warm or cold water. Which is best? Why? Do we need anything for washing besides water?** Do a simple experiment to see whether soap lathers best in hot or cold water.

It may sometimes happen in an integrated topic such as this that the focus moves away from RE. That's not necessarily a bad thing, provided the class experience RE-led topics as well. It is expected that recording and display work illustrate the whole topic, not just the RE part.

INTEGRATED TOPIC: Symbols

Why do it?

● Symbols are all around us and we need to be able to interpret them.

● Symbols of different sorts are central to the great world faiths.

BACKGROUND

You may wish to distinguish between signs and symbols. This isn't easy, as definitions vary. We suggest that as working definitions for infants you describe signs as things that give instructions or directions and symbols as standing for something that may not always be obvious (for example, the owl as a symbol of wisdom). Use road signs as examples of instructions or directions. In the case of religion, symbols include faith identity 'badges'. But some faiths – Judaism, Islam and Protestant Christianity – are very cautious about using symbols, and would not use statues or pictures of people in their worship on the grounds that this would break the commandment (in the Jewish Bible, the Christian Old Testament and the Muslim Qur'an) against idolatry – the making or worship of images.

Starting points

Work on road signs and road safety.

Looking at a religious object. Try to obtain three of the following objects. (More may confuse.) Choose from a Buddha statue, a crucifix, a Hindu god statue, a picture of Guru Nanak or Guru Gobind Singh

A portrait of Guru Nanak, the founder of Sikhism, in a gurdwara in Coventry

Buddhism

Hinduism

Judaism

Christianity

Islam

Sikhism

(Sikhism); plus, from the 'no image' faiths, either a Muslim prayer mat containing a picture of Makkah (Mecca), or a Jewish prayer shawl. All of these will be obtainable from RE Centres, county or LEA collections, the museum service or postal agencies that sell artefacts (see advertisements in *RE Today*, referred to in Further Reading, p.60). Sometimes 'junk' shops sell some of these artefacts second-hand quite cheaply.

Try

Conceal the chosen objects so that they can be produced one at a time as required. Start by showing the children an ordinary photograph. **This isn't the real person, but it's an image or a reflection of the person. It reminds us about the person. If it is someone we like, we take care of the photo and don't rip it up. In religion X, person Y is very important** (produce the first object) **but no one really knows what he looked like. Why do you think they've drawn him like that?** (E.g. to look kind, wise, strong, brave.) **In religion Z, people don't think it's right to make or draw these sorts of pictures, but they use other things, like this** (show the second object, the prayer mat, for example). **All these things are called symbols because they stand for something.**

Many Muslims have their own prayer mats which are decorated with intricate patterns and may contain a picture of Makkah.

The Hindu god Shiva is often represented in statues as the Lord of the Dance.

Jewish men wear a prayer shawl (called a tallit) when they pray.

Follow-up

Discuss the idea of identity, and badges that show 'belonging'. Examples are school badges, team badges and colours, hobby badges, religious badges. **They remind us that we belong to something and they tell other people. But belonging isn't just about wearing a badge. It's about doing things.** Develop a secular example (perhaps Brownies or Cubs) and a religious example.

The men in this picture are Sikhs. As Sikhs, they have to get up early each morning to say their prayers. When they get dressed they wear five special things which are symbols of their religion.

For any of these topics it is possible to create a self-assessment sheet. The FARE Project provided several models, two of which are reproduced on the following pages by kind permission. One aims to assess performance, the other enjoyment.

Sikhs wear the Five Ks as symbols of their faith. They are: kesh (uncut hair, often covered by a turban), kanga (comb), karah (steel wrist band), kaccha (under-shorts) and kirpan (sword).

R E ACTIVITY
SELF-ASSESSMENT SHEET

These sheets are introduced at the beginning of the topic, and completed as each activity is finished or at the end of the topic.

The criteria for self-assessment are carefully explained to the children so they can assess their own work. These criteria are deliberately kept simple:

> I think I did this job very well

> I could have done this job better

> I didn't do this job very well

The RE activity sheet is used as a method of recording this assessment. The child draws a smiley, plain or frowny face in the first, second or third boxes as appropriate. There is room for teacher comment/assessment if required. The completed sheets can then be the basis for individual discussions with each child. They are part of the learning process, and provide part of the evidence for teacher assessment. The child can choose a piece or pieces of work to be kept with/attached to the sheet.

Examples are given for two topics. In each case, sections of relevant Programmes of Study and Specific Objectives have been chosen to demonstrate links with the framework.

1   Activity self-assessment sheet   Creation

2   Activity self-assessment sheet   People who help us

An alternative way of incorporating self-assessment for a single piece of work is to explain the criteria to the children as above, and ask them to draw the appropriate face at the bottom of their work.

EXAMPLE 1

ACTIVITY
SELF-ASSESSMENT SHEET

CREATION

Aims

To introduce the word "creation".

To read creation stories from Judaeo-Christian and other sources.

To explore man-made and natural creations.

Programmes of study

Pupils should be given the opportunity to:

A experience and respond to the natural world.

  hear some religious stories of the natural world and of creation.

B develop their sense of enquiry and curiosity.

  talk about questions which result from their thinking about life, relationships and the natural world, and possible answers to these questions, including answers from different religious traditions.

Specific objectives

A6 Pupils should know something of the power, beauty and cruelty of the natural world.

A7 Pupils should be familiar with some religious stories of the natural world and of creation.

B1 Pupils should be aware that there are many puzzling questions about life.

B3 Pupils should be aware that people answer questions of meaning in different ways, some of which are religious.

CREATION

	😀	😐	☹️
Name			
Create a new animal			
The first person story			
Written work I think the most beautiful thing in the world is …			
Pick and draw a daisy			
Environmental poster			
Teacher comment			

KEY STAGE 1

Name............

Harvest

Draw

Is there anything you did NOT enjoy?

Tell your teacher

Draw

something special you remember

FOLD

---

think

Did you enjoy the Harvest Assembly?

Fill in

? ? ?
I am not sure

I enjoyed it

I did NOT enjoy it

PITS AND HOW NOT TO FALL INTO THEM

Secularising religious material

Sometimes hours of work by teacher and class, leading to magnificent art, drama, discussion and imaginative work are poured into what appears to be an RE topic, only to be shown on closer inspection to have no RE in it at all. How can this happen? It occurs when teachers remove from the story or topic the religious frame of reference and thus turn the material into something else, something totally secular. These are some examples from old favourites in the classroom:

● It happens when the Joseph story (Genesis 37, 39 to 50) is told without any of the thirty-eight references to God in the Hebrew Bible/Old Testament version. Far from 'any dream will do', as the musical version has it, this story seeks to emphasize that not only does God communicate through dreams, but that the ability to interpret them correctly is a gift from God too. Any dream just won't do!

● It happens when the story of Samson (Judges 13 to 16) has its thirty references to God removed in the telling, in which he then becomes a hunky torso man (Incredible Bible Hulk?) whose body is much stronger than his intelligence.

● It happens when God, who is referred to seven times in the much shorter story of David and Goliath (I Samuel 17), disappears in the retelling.

● And it happens when the good Samaritan (Luke 10:25–37) becomes merely a kind man to someone found after a mugging. The connection with the commandment (verse 27) and the fact that to many Jews of the time the only 'good' Samaritan was a dead one (a feeling matched only by that of the Samaritans for the Jews), is ignored as the story becomes a secular twentieth-century moralism about helping people in need. But in the real story, the religious expert almost choked rather than name a Samaritan as hero (verse 37).

Why do teachers edit out God and religion, thus making unrecognisable so much profoundly religious material? They wouldn't dream of censoring or mangling history or science by taking out vital pieces of information that help children to interpret evidence. It may be that God is thought of as too hard for infants. This may be because many teachers were trained in the shadow of Ronald Goldman's research work of the mid 1960s, in which he applied Piagetian analysis of the conceptual development of children to RE. This was taken to mean that one did not deal with 'abstract' ideas in the early years, but relied on themes such as bread, light, water, and so on.

Perhaps late twentieth-century society in Britain finds 'God' an embarrassing topic among adults, or maybe teachers can't quite feel their way in to the right sort of language about God, without thinking that they are somehow indoctrinating the children. In fact, one is indoctrinating the children by censoring God out of the story too. Omitting God creates a more serious problem of indoctrination because it isn't obvious to the child that anything has been removed.

Approaches to RE

Here, then, are some approaches to talking to infants about God that don't compromise the integrity of the teacher or the child.

The children in front of us will already have acquired different ideas and vocabulary about God without our help and outside our classroom. They will tend to state their views on God and God's actions rather than ask teachers about them, though the death of a pet or a person sometimes prompts questions about what God is or is not doing about it. Their picture of God will be anthropomorphic, the jargon way of saying that they will talk about and imagine God to be like a human being, who sees, hears, speaks, perhaps like we do, or pops up from nowhere to censure people like the head teacher does! Or he may be seen as a heavenly Father Christmas – distant, elderly, kind, slightly unreal, quite likes children.

It is hardly surprising that God should be seen in this way by Key Stage 1 children; indeed it would be surprising if 'he' – to use anthropomorphic and possibly sexist language again – were thought of in any other way. Problems arise for older children and adults who cannot see how to move on from this phase without necessarily rejecting belief in God altogether, or if they fail to see that anthropomorphisms can be used cleverly by and for adults, as in the Garden of Eden story (Genesis 3), for instance.

We can also distinguish between reception class and top infants in their ability to 'handle' God. Reception will cheerfully muddle God and Jesus or the central figure of their own religious tradition, with the possible exception of Islam, which constantly emphasizes that Prophet Muhammad is neither God, nor God's son. The world the reception class child inhabits is prepared to accept fairies, frogs who turn into princes, magicians, princesses who marry beasts, and so on because in this world there is no need to distinguish between story and history, science and fantasy. They may be able to distinguish these if prompted by the teacher, but left alone tend not to raise them as issues. Even the child who tells you in class that there aren't any witches, may be frightened to go to bed at home in case there's one in the bedroom.

But the top infant questions more. They may ask without prompting, 'Did it "really" happen?', 'How did she do it?', 'Where did he come from?', etc. It is the start of the road that leads to the adult debate about whether God belongs to the world of fantasy or of history or of story or of science or of technology.

But when God is there, there in the story, we have no right to edit 'him' out. We would find it very objectionable in adult conversation if we heard someone telling one of our favourite stories that we 'dine out on' without mentioning us; it wouldn't be the same story any more. It would be rather like turning Macbeth into a marriage guidance case study! So it is better for teachers not to fidget with God when 'he' appears in stories, not to be awkward, not to assume pious or embarrassed tones, but to deal with God matter of factly.

> 'God said to Moses ...' (He certainly did, in the story.)

Or, if it is preferable,

> 'Moses believed that he could hear God telling him to ...' (Moses did believe this, whether we accept the idea of God or not.)

Or put another way, if we don't want to appear to be pushing God,

> 'The story says that God ...', which still allows the story to make its claim without censorship of its central point. The teacher can use this device to let the story speak for itself and to distance herself and her beliefs or disbeliefs from it.

Discussion

As early as the top infants class, teachers can enter into follow-up conversation about the children's response. How do you think God 'said' it? Is it different from how I talk to you? etc. Their answers will show division between those who think it was a 'real' – i.e. external, recordable – voice and those who think 'It was in Moses' head'. Children who are beginning to realise that they can read in their head and speak or sing in their head, are not far from realising that other things might occur in their head.

By being prepared to question and discuss, teachers will be helping older infants to ask questions that will lead them to a more sophisticated understanding of the idea of God, for educationally speaking 'God' is a shorthand term that means different things to different people. Certainly already by top infants the children will switch off if they sense the odour of piety or the whiff of assembly moralisms arising in RE topics or God conversation in class.

With reception class the teacher accepts their own basic views on their level, and can ask, 'How do you think God felt when ...?' This is simply accepting the discussion on their wavelength and on the terms of the story, not perjuring one's own possible agnosticism or atheism. Nor is it indoctrinating children, for they brought these views into the classroom, and it would be strange if the 5 per cent approximately of school time devoted to RE somehow 'beat' the 95 per cent of secular assumptions and indoctrination behind the rest of the curriculum, though the values that underlie the 95 per cent seem to trouble teachers less and are less often debated.

Another way of keeping the discussion open is to emphasize, even with infants, that 'Some think this, others think that ...' or 'What do you think?', or even – and they will accept this when it is not done patronisingly – 'That would be very hard to explain to you now, but when you're older ...' or 'We don't know the answer to these questions for sure because ...'

Avoiding censorship
It is a *fact* that members and adherents of the world's religions believe that God is real and active and that *belief* affects their lives; these people are probably a large majority, taking the planet as a whole. That does not make them right, of course, in their belief. But beliefs matter, whether they are secular beliefs, about animal rights or equal opportunities or green issues, for instance, or religious beliefs, about God, life beyond this one, etc.

What right have we as teachers, living in one tiny island on the planet – an island in which unbelief might be currently the fashion – to avoid all talk of God in our classroom? That would be a strange censorship. What we need instead is to conduct God-talk honestly and sensitively, to keep doors open for children to decide for themselves when they're older. They have the right to decide and that implies the right to be aware of both sides of the case.

TO THINK ABOUT

'It's adults who've got problems about God, not children ...'

'Before anyone can talk about whether they believe in God, they've got to have some sort of idea of the God they're supposed to be believing in or disbelieving in. That's what they ought to be discussing first, their idea of God.'

'You can get too hung up on the word "God". Start by looking at what it means to people ...'

'Listen to the youngsters on this subject. They can teach us ...'

(Views expressed by students in training)

RE is everywhere (and nowhere?) in my teaching

The real experience of many infant children in RE is rather bitty. They do it with Mrs X, but not with Mrs Y, as they move up the school conveyer belt. Why? The chances are that you as a teacher overhear Mrs Y in the staffroom saying that she doesn't believe in God and so she isn't going to do RE in her class. We have already seen (p.7) that this view is based on a misunderstanding of what RE is about, also on a misunderstanding of the rights of children (p.9) and that this sort of disposal of RE is quite illegal and wide open to parental complaint or inspector's criticism (p.11). Mrs Y may realise this too, and this could lead to her claim that RE is 'everywhere' or that 'it comes into everything'. A passing inspector or interested parent is therefore entitled to ask how it is being delivered in Technology. Or Science? Or Music? Let me see your records to see how it 'came into' today's lessons. The legal reality is that Mrs Y's class are entitled to RE. If she is going to decline to teach it, the head teacher must make arrangements for someone else to do it.

We knew a very talented Mrs Y, who used to tell fairy stories and then 'unpack' them. Her 'Goldilocks and the Three Bears' played to packed houses and the children demanded retellings. If only she'd made the film of the story! Her analysis was magical: What did Goldilocks' behaviour show about her? How would you feel if you were Baby Bear? What do you feel when people interfere with your food? Should girls on their own enter strange houses? It was a gem. Well worth doing. Well worth doing again. But not RE. There was no 'R' in it. Unlike the stories that we saw on p.52 that had religion edited out, this had been selected quite deliberately because religion was never in it. It is simply good Personal and Social Education and Mrs Y's class have done no RE.

It isn't that Mrs Y shouldn't be doing Goldilocks. She should be doing RE as well – and like so many Mrs Ys, she has shown evidence of the capacity to tell and 'unpack' stories that is so useful in RE. She can do RE too. The real difficulty is that, because of her prejudices about what RE is about, Mrs Y will never pick up a book about teaching it unless teachers reading this one help her!

SENSITIVE SUBJECT, SENSITIVE PARENTS

Any subject that deals with personal issues or life and death questions or the meaning of the universe is bound to excite comment: sometimes from people who are convinced that they know all the answers – which don't coincide with 'what Mrs X said in class today' – and sometimes from people who hear at second hand something you've said and then rise in indignation about it, usually before they have had chance to hear your side first. Seasoned infant teachers can always detect in the cloakroom after school the look in the eyes of the mum who has come to do battle! In RE, parental concerns can usually be categorised into one of three areas:

(a) Parents from a sectarian background who exercise their legal right to withdraw their children from RE, basically because they do not accept your credentials to teach the subject to their children, unless you happen to be a member of that sect. The most common example of this in RE is the Jehovah's Witnesses, but Exclusive Brethren and others find much to appal them in modern education beyond RE, such as the use of computers.

(b) Parents from a variety of religious backgrounds, and from none, who are concerned about multi-faith RE. This is sometimes because they fear that their child might catch another faith and somehow be contaminated, like catching a cold, but more often because they fear a 'multi-faith mishmash' that will reduce all faiths to the same level, in the end treating none properly, and trivialising their own faith in the process.

(c) Parents from particular types of Christian background with concerns about Satanism and desperate to avoid anything that might encourage children's interest in it by, for instance, 'celebrating' Hallowe'en in school. Their concerns are just as likely to focus on ghost poems or stories in English as on RE.

Jehovah's Witnesses

The *beliefs* of Jehovah's Witnesses are different from those of all other religious groups, but their *attitude to RE* is similar to that of other exclusivist religious groups, that is groups who have arrived at the view that they hold the truth exclusively, which is another way of saying that the rest of us are wrong.

Jehovah's Witnesses originated in the USA in the latter part of the nineteenth century. Their aim was to be faithful to the Bible, from which they believed 'mainstream Christianity' had lapsed. This Bible emphasis led them to reject the celebration of Christmas and birthdays – the Bible doesn't command these 'pagan' festivals to be held – but Witnesses can and do give presents as signs of affection at any time. The Bible forbids the eating of meat with blood in it, or the consumption of blood in any other way, because in ancient Hebrew society the blood of an animal was held to be its life essence and in Temple sacrifice it was the pouring of the life blood that mattered more than the act of killing the animal, or burning bits of the carcase. For this reason Witnesses reject blood transfusions, because to them it is like taking the other person's essence or spirit into you, though there is some debate about this among Witnesses.

Their interpretation of the Bible leads them to go out in twos, like Jesus sent his disciples, to spread the Word, and to expect a real end to this world order, after a cataclysmic battle called Armageddon, described in the book of Revelation. The date of Armageddon has been predicted to be 1914 and subsequently various other dates, including 1975 and 1984. The fact that it does not arrive leads Witnesses to think that their calculations rather than the expectation itself are at fault. After time ends, people of goodwill will inhabit the planet, ruled over from heaven by Christ and his 144,000 faithful Witnesses.

Witnesses therefore want to give religious instruction and nurture to their own children, because they assume that what you are doing in RE with the class is religious instruction, telling children what to believe. It is sometimes the case that when Witnesses know that you are not trying to indoctrinate their children into some wrong view of Christianity, as they see it, they are happy for them to be part of RE. It is certainly worth trying to explain what you are (and aren't) doing in RE to Witness parents.

One year with older children we 'did' Christmas in three murals: pagan or pre-Christian items, such as the yule log and the everlasting tree; what the Bible says; and later legend, such as the fourth wise man. Witness parents were very happy for their children to be part of that work, because it was emphasizing what they see as central – that Christmas as it stands is not entirely biblical, nor obligatory, since Christianity existed for its first 300 years without celebrating it at all.

It will always be disappointing to teachers who want their class to be a family in which diversity of home, culture and religion is affirmed and celebrated and in which we can learn from one another without losing our integrity or identity, when any parent pulls the legal cord of withdrawal, but until that area of law is seen to be an anachronism, the right lies with the parent to act in this way. If an issue in RE arises spontaneously in class, however, through questions the children ask, as it can very often in the infant classroom, DES Circular 3/89 points out that teachers are not expected to rush to put 'withdrawn' children in the cupboard or out of the way somewhere! We are asked instead to show professional sensitivity towards the reasons for which the child has been withdrawn.

Parents' fears about multi-faith material

The fears of parents and their underlying reasons for fears about multi-faith material vary. In some cases the underlying reason might be racism: we don't want our child to learn about 'these immigrants' pagan religions', etc. In other cases sometimes Christians or Muslims or parents from other faiths fear that by teaching various faiths, we are somehow transmitting the value that they are equally true, when they would argue that they have found the full truth, or perhaps the only truth, in one of them. Sometimes parents fear that teachers are engaged in a facile window-shopping approach to religion – find a faith you like and wear it! Religion as a 'pic'n'mix'.

This is not a book about the philosophy of RE, and so we must be content with a very compressed answer here to help infant teachers deal with these issues if they arise.

1. The law requires us to teach about the main faiths present in the UK.

2. When these faiths are present in our school, it becomes a natural part of learning about one another and our local community.

3. Even where they are not present and the school is 'Christian' or nothing, there are good educational reasons for learning about the way of life of other human beings, both in the UK and in the wider world.

4. It is not our business, certainly with infants, to go into whether one faith is 'better' or 'truer' than others, or whether they are equally true, or for that matter, equally untrue. Our task is to show that

they are sincerely believed in, and in that sense alive, and to show that they affect the daily lives of their members and adherents, including young children.

5. We may need to make clear to parents why we are teaching world faiths, and to convey our professional view that to nurture children into a particular faith is the province of home and family, mosque, synagogue, church, etc. Nothing we do in school will seek to undermine that, where it is occurring, but nurture in a particular faith is properly the concern of the home.

Fears about Satanism

One of the things that a number of world faiths agree about is the reality of evil. Many non-Muslims will not know that one of the reasons why Muslims find *The Satanic Verses* so objectionable is that it appears to identify or at least to see no difference between good and evil. To non-religious people, evil may seem rather comic, like those cartoons of the horned red devil, complete with tail and trident.

To conservative believers in several faiths, that is grossly under-estimating the evil power, which they see at work in modern society in various forms. Anything that turns these powers into a joke, strengthens them and their chance of making people captive. Therefore anything – Hallowe'en, ouija boards, ghost stories, whatever – that trivialises them may be helping evil to advance and encouraging experimentation with spirits.

Not all teachers will, of course, agree with this view, but it is important to understand the passion with which it is held. There may well be agreed syllabus or LEA rules or guidelines about such topics. Teachers would be advised to check these, and to enquire into the strength of feeling about these matters in their school parent body, before embarking on work in this field. Infant head teachers may find themselves being lobbied by 'pro' and 'anti' parents and staff on issues such as ghostly material. But in any case in RE there are so many festivals in different faiths to which these fears cannot be applied, that there is plenty to choose from without going for controversy!

FURTHER READING

To use in class

A Gift to the Child: Religious Education in the Primary School by M.Grimmitt, J.Grove, J.Hull and L.Spencer, 1991, Teacher's Source Book (Simon & Schuster), 14 pupils' books and audio cassette. This teaching pack is a result of the Religion in the Service of the Child (RISC) Project undertaken in Birmingham schools. The Project team produced teaching materials on seven religious items, some crossing more than one faith: Our Lady of Lourdes; Ganesha; Nanak's song; the Call to Prayer; Angels; Jonah; Hallelujah. The 136 page teacher's source book provides the sort of context and approaches to the items which teachers will welcome. Despite the title, the focus is infant rather than junior.

World faiths stories, written by members of the faiths and illustrated for young children, published by Wayland, include:

Hindu Stories by V.P.Hemant Kanitkar (1986). This includes Ganesha.

The Life of the Buddha by John Snelling (1987) – includes the material referred to in Chapter 4.

The Life of Muhammad by Maryam Davies (1987) – includes the story of the spider's web, used in Chapter 4.

Guru Nanak and the Sikh Gurus by Ranjit Arora (1987) – includes material on Guru Hargobind.

Stories from the Hindu World by Jamila Gavin (Macdonald, 1986), contains the story of Manu's ark and how Lord Agni tried to hide, both referred to in Chapter 4.

Seasons of Splendour by Madhur Jaffrey (Puffin, 1992), is a rich collection of Indian material told for older children, but of use to infant teachers. It contains the Hindu Divali story referred to in Chapter 4.

For material on festivals there is the book of that name by Beverley Birch (Macdonald, 1984). Good source material for teachers is contained in ***High Days and Holidays*** by Margaret Joy (Faber, 1981), ***Festive Occasions*** by Judy Ridgway (OUP, 1986), ***Ramadan and Eid ul Fitr*** by Olive Bennett (Macmillan Educational, 1986) and ***Divali*** by Chris Deshpande (A & C Black, 1984).

Experienced teachers will scan the children's shelves of good public libraries for similar books, using the pictures with infants where the text needs retelling in their language. If possible, check that the writer comes from the faith community involved or has taken steps to check their material with members of it.

Background reading for the teacher who knows nothing about world faiths

Religions by Alan Brown, John Rankin and Angela Wood (Longman, 1988)

Six Religions in the 20th Century by W.Owen Cole (Hulton, 1986). He wrote *Five World Faiths* (Cassell, 1984). Buddhism is the added sixth!

Owen Cole's book **Come inside the Church** visits places of worship in six religions, with illustrations (not photographs), (Studio Vista, 1974).

For the teacher wishing to use material from the Qur'an, there are various English translations or paraphrases, available in good bookshops. One with an index is essential for those unfamiliar with the text. We used the translation by Muhammad Zafrulla Khan (Curzon Press, 1971).

For the teacher who knows nothing about the Bible, read: **The Bible: the Story of the Book** by Terence Copley (Bible Society, 1990). Fifty basic questions about the Bible and its origins are dealt with.

To use in assessment

The Main Report of the FARE Project, 1991 (in libraries, but available for purchase only from the FARE Office, University of Exeter School of Education, St Luke's, Heavitree Road, Exeter EX1 2LU, £12.00 including postage). This includes 33 pages of photocopiable examples specifically for Key Stage 1, free of copyright to purchasers.

To keep up to date with the latest RE resources

Enrol in membership of PCfRE, the Professional Council for RE. This entitles the school to the termly magazine *RE Today*, written by and for serving teachers and including reviews of all the latest materials for classroom use in RE, as well as a wall poster and often a cover that can be cut out and turned into a second poster. A Worship File also includes ideas for collective worship ('assemblies'). With this can come a primary mailing of further classroom-related materials. All this is also available without PCfRE membership. For details contact: PCfRE, Royal Buildings, Victoria Street, Derby DE1 1GW.